EVENT THERAPY

10 Steps to Ultimate Event Planning

Charessa Sawyer, MSW

Event Therapist

Edited by Shakeema Bouyer & Uvonda Willis
Cover Design by Charessa Sawyer
Published by Still Standing Publishing, LLC

Printed in the United States of America

ISBN-13:978-1986646147
ISBN-10:1986646149

Acknowledgements

I am truly grateful that I was given the push to write this book. The first of many books that will focus on understanding the craft of event planning and what it takes to not only be financially successful, but also mentally capable to walk the journey.

I dedicate this accomplishment to my mother, Barbara, for pushing me to simply step out on faith and go forward no matter my challenges. She explained to me that I could do and be anything that I have set in my heart.

God is the foundation of each and every one of my accomplishments and I am grateful for whatever is to come for me.

I would like to thank my event team, past and present. Without them having my back and helping to build my event company, I would not be on this amazing and glorious journey!

Finally, I would like to thank my client, Tamiko

Lowry Pugh, who has seriously turned into a mentor in many ways. She gave me the final push to birth this dream of mine. She allowed God to use her to support me. I am forever grateful and honored that God made a way for our paths to cross.

Testimonials

Just back from attending the Event Therapy Circle Ultimate Event Workshop! It was the ultimate event and I learned so much from the experts!
– Kimberly O., Student

What an awesome experience at the Event Therapy Workshop. I can't wait to pick up the book.
– Courtney S., Student

Charessa is a real boss and team leader! She knows how to motivate and teach you. She also knows and understands the business, and I have seen her share her knowledge and expertise with others. She is definitely someone you want to watch in the event industry.
– Sierra R., COO of SC Visionary Services

Important Note to Readers

The information presented in this book is for informational and educational purposes only. It is intended to motivate and inspire you to take proper steps to achieving your business goals while managing your emotions. Any advice or suggestions provided are not intended to be the only way of building your business. Always be sure to consult with your lawyer, accountant or business coach to help you properly develop your business.

Key strategies and resources discussed to help reduce stress are some of many ways to support your goal. In the coming editions, we will provide more detailed strategies for the purpose of managing emotions.

Table of Contents

Introduction

A Guide for Understanding & Embracing the Steps to Developing a Successful Event Business in a Crowded Forest of Planners.

"Never stop being a student of your profession."

-Simply Charessa

Event Planning is soooo fun! Well, at least for some of us it is. The reason event planning and production is so fun is because we have found a method to the madness. Every person believes he or she can put together an event; but one must ask - Do I have the steps to put together a successful event that guests rave about for years to come? Is my mind clear? Are my pockets happy?

I for one have learned many, many lessons over the years. Although, I have had ups and downs, the encouraging part is that I have acquired

essential steps to ensure the ups trump the downs. The one lesson that has resonated with me is simply BE YOURSELF. The purpose of this workbook is to provide you with a sense of ease via 10 Steps to Ultimate Event Planning!

We will share helpful information and template worksheets that will give you an understanding of the event planning process; whether you are producing events as the host or producing an event for a client. We have also included key therapeutic strategies to help develop an event business that meets the heart of a client and reduces stress or overwhelming feelings.

Whether it is special events, cause-based events or weddings, all event types follow similar steps. Each event coordinator or planner should have a business plan, identify a niche market, develop an efficient team and lists of vendors, etc., to run a successful event business. The templates and worksheets in this book are going to be fundamental as you get started!

After each chapter, there are questions for you to answer. Ask yourself what you have learned from the chapter? What you will change for your next event, who are you targeting and of course, am I making money to cover my business, my team and myself?

Let's get started!!

Event Therapy
Provides strategies, motivation and resources that support and inspire eventpreneurs in mentally managing events and achieving their goals.
-Simply Charessa

STEP 1
We All have a Gift...Identify It!

This chapter will help you focus and understand who, what and why you are getting into the event business.

To get started, take 5 minutes to think about your event business. Who are you targeting? Why are you targeting them? What is your purpose and your role in the event industry?

The most powerful thing about being a business owner is your uniqueness. Everyone has a gift that can transpose into a business that supports others. Before starting your business, you must identify this. What is it about me that I love and others will love as well? What is it about me that can help someone solve their problems? What is it about me that can meet the need of others? In therapy, this is what we call self-identification.

According to Bing.com, the proper definition of self- identification is "the attribution of certain characteristics or qualities to oneself". So, we must step back and identify our characteristics as we think about the type of business that we will marry for better or for worse.

List 5 characteristics or qualities about yourself.

1.

2.

3.

4.

5.

Now that you have self-identified and decided that event planning is your direction, let's think about what you are good at in the industry and what you feel good doing?

There are several types of event planning that you may want to consider as your specialty. Having a specialty that your customers can identify helps position you as an expert in that area. Think about doctors. You wouldn't go to a general family doctor for a serious heart issue. You would connect with a cardiologist who specializes in this area. This is the same for your business. We know that we have the skills to plan and produce all styles of events, but what will give you the most joy and help clients identify your business in the sea of other planning businesses?

What do you like most about event planning?

1. _____
2. _____
3. _____

I can tell you that I love lights, cameras and action-packed events! I love developing the idea for the event and taking care all the logistics. Events are movies for me. I see everything holistically first, and then I can break it down into parts. I am visually creative, so again for me, it's producing and directing a movie for the premiere! I just got excited thinking about it.

When you think about events and event planning, what excites you? Keep in mind that what excites you may not be the only thing that you can do for your business, but it keeps you in the game. If you know that you do not like spray painting and crafting pieces, but you decide that you will focus on event designing, then you are setting yourself up for **event warfare.** Event warfare is constantly being engaged in conflict with your business, your clients and simply your mind. Happy planner = happy client. However, be cautious of settling or trying to choose a specialty or target population because "that's where the money is." We all love and desire money, but we should be mindful of how to include happiness in the equation. This will keep your clients contacting you.

How do I identify my target population?

Now that you know what you like and dislike about event planning and have identified your focus, think about what audience will support your specialty.

For example, my background is in therapy services. I have Masters of Social Work and I absolutely love working with people and helping them minimize and sometimes, solve their problems; however, I have found that I really enjoy interactive therapy where clients can work and learn from each other. I have also learned that entertainment is key for not just them, but for most people in the world, so I decided that I wanted to combine the love that I have for event management, entertainment and therapy to "produce events that make sense." Therefore, my target populations are philanthropists, nonprofits, government agencies, entertainers, etc. who are looking to host cause and corporate events.

ETC Diagram 1:

WHO: Who would enjoy my services?	WHO: Who would I enjoy working for? (Your client is your employer)
Answer:	Answer:
WHAT: What type of event vision will you enjoy?	WHAT: What type of services will the client enjoy?
ANSWER:	ANSWER:
WHEN: When are my targeted clients likely to need services?	WHEN: When are my services most likely available?
ANSWER:	ANSWER:

WHERE: Where do my target clients reside?	WHERE: Where will my services be provided?
ANSWER:	ANSWER:
WHY: Why are clients most likely to choose events services?	WHY: Why would clients choose my services?
ANSWER:	ANSWER:
HOW: How much are clients willing to spend?	HOW: How much are my services?
ANSWER:	ANSWER:

Once you have answered these questions, you should have a better idea of your target population and your special event market. As you may have noticed, I have yet to share the step to create your legal business entity. This is because it is important to understand what you are getting into before you create a legal business entity. First, I would like you to understand your market and identify your place in the event industry. The steps that I am providing you will help with the development of your business plan.

Note: A business plan is a legal live document that lays out future business goals, objectives and strategies for achieving them.

Resource: www.liveplans.com

How do you create your niche event market?

Once you've identified business specializations and your target population this means that you are also on the road of identifying your niche market. Your niche market is a small, specific segment of your target population that you can create by identifying needs, wants or desires that are not being or rarely being addressed by others in the industry. To satisfy this segment, your event business will develop services or products to satisfy that need.

(www.en.wikipedia.org/wiki/Target_market)

A fundamental component of creating your niche market is placing yourself in your customer's shoes.

Think about this. *Steve Jobs found that working people, especially entrepreneurs like us, were always on the go. We needed a gadget that would have the ability to make calls, access the internet and schedule activities quickly. He was able to create a product specifically for the working business population. Steve Jobs' company, Apple, niche market became men and women who worked and had a business. The development of the Apple iPhone for the market was an obvious hit because today smartphones simply rule the world of entrepreneurs.*

What you see here is that Steve Jobs was able to think outside of the box and create product that was, I think perfect for people like you and I.

For your event business, is there a need that you would like to address? Are there event services that you wish you would have been able to access as a customer? What do your current clients ask you about more often than some?

Answering these questions are amazing for your potential client because it solves their problems. Solving problems will attract potential clients to your company. Remember that I shared that the most important way to have a viable business or service is to be able to solve problems or meet the need of your clients or customer.

Take the next few minutes to take an inventory of your current client roster. If you do not have clients now that is fine, create a list of services that you feel will meet the needs of your target population.

Note: Be comfortable answering the question: How may I help you? Be Ready to share 3 top ways that you can help or solve their problems.

Exercise 1: "How may I help you?"

Take Time to write down your response to the client.

Event Planner: Hi there! How may I help you?

Potential Client: I have a vision to produce a 200 person Gala that will provide 3 college scholarships to teenage fathers. I am not certain how to make my vision reality.

Event Planner: (Note Top 3 Answers)

1).

2).

3).

Diagram 2: How to Identify Target Populations

Use the following checklist to get you started. Try to list or describe your target population in the blank boxes add other traits.

Age	Gender	Place Of Residence	Personality
Level Of Education	Career	Annual Income	Leisure Activities
Online Presence	Shopping Behavior	Other	Other

Exercise 2: Self - Identification

Most people do not take the time to think about what they like or enjoy most. They also do not think too deeply about what others would say that they like, enjoy or are good at. Here is your chance to identify with what you enjoy about yourself. Being able to self identify helps you to discover your niche.

Instructions: Complete the 20 sentences about yourself.

- I like myself because…
- I enjoy event planning because…
- I love when…
- My family tell me that I have an amazing…
- I feel amazing when…
- I feel amazing about…
- I'm an expert at…
- My favorite color is… because it makes me feel…
- My favorite place is…
- I'm loved by…
- People say I am a good…
- I like…most about event planning
- After an event, I feel…

- What I enjoy most is...
- My team would say that I am...
- I have a natural talent for...
- Goals for my future are...
- I know I will reach my goals because I am...
- People compliment me about...
- I've been successful at...

Event Therapy

Write the Vision and Make It Plain- Every Event Must First Start with a Blueprint.

STEP 2
Build It & They
Will Come

What are the steps to build your event business?

We will stray away from getting into the legalities in this section, but we will share basic event business startup. In the previous chapter, you learned to fully understand your business and your focus market. Here, we will discuss developing your goals for your business, the importance of mentors and basic steps to getting started.

The running theme for this entire book is *Be Yourself*. However, *be yourself* can easily be misinterpreted. Let's talk about this.

Creating an event business should be unique to your target population and you should have goals that will grow your business. The growth of your business starts at your business name and DBA ("Doing Business As"). You must have a unique name before begin taking steps to become a legal business entity. Unique means that the business name is your own and is not confused with other business. Unique does not mean that your market does not understand what the business name means, cannot spell or pronounce it. For example, I would advise you not to call your business "The Abracadabra Firm." First, it took me a while just to spell it correctly and even though Google helped me, I am still not confident. Secondly, it is difficult to spell, pronounce for some and it does not tell me what type of firm. I would assume it's a firm for magicians...but for magicians to do what...well I don't know.

Create a name that tells your audience who you are, what you do and sets you up as a professional entity. Some planners choose to include their name; i.e. The Barbara S. Event Planning & Design Agency.

Let's see if this name answers our test questions

Who? Barbara S.

What do they do? Event Planning & Design

Professional? Yes

If you are wondering whether you chose the best name for your business, then it is always great to consult with your Small Business Administration. The SBA usually has mentorship programs to assist you in developing your business. I would also suggest researching professional event companies to check their names, connect with a marketing company and find other organizations that provide business resources.

Let's discuss mentorship.

Exercise 3:

Tell us what you need help with:

1:_____

2:_____

3: _____

If you do not remember anything else from this book, please remember that the power of your network is fundamental to the lifeline of your business. Choose mentors who are not just event planners, but also those who are in other areas of business. Think about what is needed for your business to grow. Think about what you need to learn. I will share a few types of mentors that you may want to consider.

1. Accountant or Business Strategist
2. Lawyer or Law Professionals
3. Marketing and Public Relations Professionals
4. Event Planning Professional
5. Life Coach

When choosing mentors, please remember you are not connecting with them to drain them of their brain cells by asking questions that only benefit you; You are building relationships with people for learning purposes. You are supporting them and they are supporting you.

Never take advantage of another person; that never works out well.

Most mentors have programs, resources, books, and services that are great for your investment.

Having a business is an investment of the mind, body and pockets. It's true...not all things are free.

You should choose your mentors very wisely. The goal is to have trusted individuals who you can learn the right way of running your business. According to Kathy Caprino Leadership column (Forbes, September 14, 2014) you should never request mentorship from a stranger. Instead you should seek mentorship from someone who is mutually familiar with you and your work ethic. A true mentor will believe in your talent and will be more than willing to support you through your journey. In addition, some of your mentors may be your trusted Board of Directors.

It is of benefit to all businesses to have a board of directors to assist in making decisions for the growth of your company.

Although it is true that you should stray away from reaching out to a stranger for mentorship, it is not a problem to have what I call "Mentor in your head." A mentor in your head is an individual who you do not know, or may not have met, but find yourself learning from that person. For example, I have always said that Tyler Perry is a mentor in my head because I have gained so much wisdom from studying his journey, reading his books and watching how he has used his faith in God to guide him along the way. Like many others, I have noted Oprah Winfrey and Michelle Obama as mentors. If you have noticed none of the three powerhouses mentioned are event planners; you must be reminded that you are able to learn many essential business values from outside of your particular field. However, I do have MINH who is a part of the event industry. Have you heard of Mindy Weis, Tony Conway, or Preston Bailey? They are all phenomenal planners and designers!

Join our Event Therapy Circle Group to network with event planning professionals

eventtherapycircle@gmail.com

Can you have too many mentors?

Well, what I will say is when creating your list of mentors, know why they are your mentor. What purpose are they serving for your business or for your professional growth? If you have 5 mentors providing advice on the same subject... well event warfare sets in again.

Note: When developing your business, be purposeful in everything you do.

Networking

You may be wondering where you are able to find mentors. One of the great ways to find mentors is by attending and supporting events or programs of those whom you are seeking mentorship. Find out how you are able to help them with their next project. Show them your hard work and skills. Those who believe in you will not mind becoming your mentor when the time is right.

Mentors sometimes happen by coincidence. Professionals who you grow to admire and grow to admire you may also be your current accountant, lawyer or business strategist. These are very valuable relationships that you want to cherish.

In my experience, one of my mentors is a production manager. She has been working in the industry for over 25 years and has produced some of the most amazing projects. After getting to know her and sharing my desire for a mentor, she shared that she would be more than happy to be a mentor. That relationship happened by coincidence, but was absolutely awesome for my growth.

Diagram 3: Below list 5 potential mentors in your database in which you would like to connect. Include their phone numbers, website and one program or product in which you would consider investment. Lastly, tell us why this person may be a great mentor.

Event Therapy Circle Mentorship Chart

Mentor Name	Area of Expertise	Phone Number	Email Address	Website	Product or Program

Now that you have your business name and you have reviewed it with your mentor, it is time to develop a business plan. Your business plan should provide summary about your business, mission, vision, core values and includes 3-5 years of a projected budget. Once your business plan has been created, you can register your business name with the state. Your lawyer or business strategist may be able to help you with this. Once you have registered your name and determined the type of business entity, i.e. LLC, LLP, S Corp, etc., you can purchase your business license and obtain business insurance(s).

Note: Every state is different. Check with a business lawyer or consultant to ensure you have taken all proper steps.

Note 2: Business liability insurance should be a requirement for all event business.

Event Therapy
Dreams don't work unless you do.
-John C Maxwell

STEP 3
How to Maintain a
Kick Ass Team

Your team is your lifeline. Creating a team with qualified individuals who are dedicated and determined is another essential step of ultimate event planning. The way to attract your team is to simply be yourself, have an identifiable niche market and support them. Many event planning teams are set up with 1-2 staff personnel and a host of interns, volunteers as well as preferred vendors.

As a small business, you may not be able to afford financing a large team of supporters, so interns are going to be very important in sustaining your business and executing your events.

Note: Be yourself and you will attract those who are relatable and like being around you.

Team Member Testimonial

SC Visionary planning & Production services is a great team to be a part of. We are a family and enjoy exceeding our clients' expectations. They are amazed at how we work together to execute their vision. Adria Sanders, Volunteer Coordinator.

There will be team members who come and those who will go, but that is a part of any business. It is important to have an open communication policy with your team. Ensure that they know your business and event goals. How your team feels is essential in how long they will stick with you. Below is a list of tips to consider when building a team.

Event Therapy Team Development Tips

1. Provide each team member with a defined role and position.
2. Have consistent face to face meetings and conference calls.
3. Have policies and procedures in which all must adhere.
4. Set team goals.
5. Be open and clear with business and event goals.

6. Communicate.
7. Have fun with each person as a group.
8. Get to know you team members.
9. Set realistic expectations.
10. Pray.

Most importantly

Delegate Delegate Delegate

Your team should be like minded individuals who can grow with you. When you delegate responsibilities and tasks that are clear, they will invest themselves in the success of the business. Again, your kick ass team is your life line. They are your motivation and you are their motivation. Support them like they support you.

Diagram 4: Event Therapy: Event Team Assignment Sheet

Team Leader	No. of Team members	Type of Event	Client Name	Date & Time	Client email
Example: Sierra R.	3 Staff 5 Volunteers	Survivor's Conference & Pink Champagne Gala	Charge Up Campaign	June 1 6:30pm June 2nd: 9:00am June 2nd (evening) 7:30pm	chargeupca mpaign@g mail.com

Communication is Key

Sometimes people have trouble accepting positive advice from others; especially those who are on their team. This is because they think the other person is telling them what to do or even judging them. No person wants to feel criticized. Most of the time, professionals are giving advice because they want you to succeed and they see something that you may not see.

Be sure to have all of the team members

understand your communication policy and feel comfortable discussing any conflict with your Human Resource Officer.

Exercise 4

Put a check next to the best way to respond to the advice given.

1. . Advice: "I think you should remove the plexiglass glass dance floor and simply use a sound stage to cover the pool to reduce the cost estimate."

   _____ "You're right. That's what I will do."

   _____ "Thanks for the advice." (walks away to leave the conversation)

   _____ "Thanks, but that does not provide the look that I am seeking."

   _____ "Thanks for the advice! Let's talk more about your suggestions and see which idea will be
   best for our client."

2. Advice: "You should probably pay your staff more to reduce the high turnover"

   _____ "What I pay my staff is not for discussion"

   _____ "That sounds like a good suggestion. Why do you think the pay is the reason for the high turnover?"

_____ "I am not concerned with high turnover."

3. Advice: "I suggest that for large scale corporate events, table vendors should only be utilized if there is a separate room to house them or they are placed where the main event is not distracted."

_____ "Hmm, let's look at the venue room diagram and see if this is a possibility."

_____ "I think they are fine where they are."

_____ "Well, I am not sure why this is an issue to discuss."

The above communication exercise on advice is important to use and understand in your business. Team members and vendors will have advice that may be against what you feel is the best solution for a problem or situation. Hearing them out and holding a positive conversation will help build your leadership and reduce potential stress in your business.

Always Remember: *Never be so learned that you cannot learn anything from others.* - Horatio Leonard, Higher Grounds Events

Never be so learned that you cannot learn anything from others.

Event Therapy

Communication is a two-way street and can be the blessing or the lesson for any business.

STEP 4
Is Public Relations & Marketing Even Necessary?

Why is PR/Advertising/ Marketing important for Event Planning Brand?

Now that you have legally formed your business, written your business plan, developed a company budget plan and built your team, you should begin marketing your business to the public and sharing with communities.

Build a website that is pretty, consistent, resourceful and simple. As a small business, you may not want to spend thousands of dollars on building a website, but you do want to make sure that your site looks professional.

Here are a few resources for you:

1. Electric Heart Media
2. Wix.com
3. Weebly.com
4. Godaddy.com

Wix and Weebly are both easy to build sites that you can do yourself or hire an intern to build. Many of these sites now host your email marketing database and provide automation! This is awesome right! Automation allows you to automatically send a potential client an email response for the services booked with you. This is important as you work to establish your event planning business brand.

Establishing your brand is another sure way to bring in clients. Event planning is heavily driven on visuals and word of mouth; therefore, you want to ensure that your business is recognizable and the chatter is positive. This includes creating a nice professional logo with your color scheme. Your color scheme will be used on all your resources, websites and your social media.

Note: *Remember when developing your brand, think about the personality of your company, your target population and your message. Your brand look will attract specific client types.*

Automation helps you to manage your time and be more efficient.

Most event planning businesses do not need or have a public relations firm to represent them, so you become your own publicist. Public relations is the practice of spreading information about your business or event to the public. It is a reactive service that is usually dependent on the marketing strategy that you have implemented. In a nutshell, whereas public relations service reacts to what your business does, marketing generates the conversation by promoting the service or brand to encourage the news necessary for public relations to then share. Now, I am not a publicist nor a marketing professional. I have gathered my understanding through research and having a lot of PR friends who represent organizations, businesses, and individuals.

According to Dr. Phillip Kotler, the purpose of marketing is to create and bring to market a product, service or brand that people will buy.

This is usually done by creating and using visuals that the market can relate to and remember.

Public Relations main purpose is to share information in efforts to build relationships with stakeholders and potential clients. This is typically done by creating press releases, pitches and etc. to deliver value about your product, service or brand that satisfies the target market. (I would suggest that you research, take PR and marketing classes as well as attend workshops so that you are familiar with these services.)

PR and Marketing are both luxury services that can be expensive. Consult with a professional to determine when it is time to secure each service for your business.

Here are other resources that may be helpful:

1. The PR Code by Lillie Mae PR
2. PR for a Day by Ronnika Ann (IGN PR)

Social Media is Lit For Event Professionals!

In today's world, social media is very important in your business. This is especially so for event designers, party planners and wedding planners. To use this amazing, free tool effectively you may hire a social media manager who will help you create memes and a pattern for your social media page. They will also maintain a consistent look and ensure proper content is being posted daily to your site. This is all a part of business branding.

Scheduling apps like HootSuite, Planoly and Buffer are your friend with social media because this amazing tool can also be time consuming and stressful. It is easy to get stuck comparing ourselves with other businesses on social media but you have to stay focused on your mission and vision. Another concern for event coaching clients is time management. Below are 2 timeless management tips:

1. Develop a social media calendar
2. Delegate social media tasks

info@scvisionaryservices.com for more information on social media event strategies.

Diagram 5: Event Therapy Circle Social Media Calendar Example

	Morning	Mid-Day	Evening
Monday	Information	No Post	Fun
Tuesday	No Post	Sales Post	Info Post
Wednesday	Engagement Post (Video)	Quote	No Post
Thursday	Sales Post	Info Post	Fun Post
Friday	Engagement Post		Video
Saturday		Sales	
Sunday			Info

Now that you have learned the basics of public relations and marketing, created your website and social media pages, you can utilize each service to help advertise your brand and to develop the ultimate event strategy.

In ultimate event planning, your key is having a well-prepared event strategy for each event that you produce. Your event strategy identifies your market and creates a connection between your target population, the event and your business. Like any business, all events begin with a mission, a vision, an objective and a strategy to reach the result. In my case, my goal is to premier an amazing event for our clients and the participants! We will talk more about this in a separate event therapy edition.

Exercise 5: Event Therapy Circle Event Strategy Development

Below is a list of 5 questions to creating an event strategy.

1. What do you want out of the event and how will you measure it?

_____

_____

2. What are your short and long-term successes?

_____

_____

3. What content can you develop about your event?

_____

_____

4. What is the budget for the overall event?

    _____

    _____

5. What can you offer that is free to engage
    your population?

    _____

    _____

6. What is your follow up plan?

    _____

    _____

These strategies are helpful for planners who are looking to host internal events or events that are planned, produced and executed for your brand and not a client and for external events.

Scenario: A bride wants to ensure that her guests are blown away at her wedding and she is holding you responsible for making this happen.

Objective- Ensure that the client and her guests are amazed at the entire wedding to include logistics and design.

Measure: You will measure by obtaining testimonials from her guests, visual reactions caught on video and photos.

Short term goal: The short-term success may be that the clients were happy, enjoyed the food, amazed at the designs and entered the wedding with ease.

Budget goal: The budget determines the design and logistics of entire wedding.

Content: The content that you will create will be the beautiful wedding invitations and save the dates that you send ahead of the wedding and the emails that you exchange with vendors.

Offer: You may offer transportation services, welcome gifts in the guest hotel rooms and party favors.

Follow Up: Your follow up plan will be thank you cards, photo booth photos and video clips sent to the guests via email.

As you see, because you created a strategy you have met the mission and vision of the wedding for the client. I am pretty sure that the guests will be blown away by the completion of these steps!

Exercise 6: Event Therapy Circle Event Strategy

List 3 key strategies that you have used.

1.

2.

3.

List strategies that you will now use to upgrade your event strategy.

1.

2.

3.

Diagram 6: Event Therapy: Event Strategy Plan

Long Term Goal	Objective	Short Term Goal	Measure
Budget	Offer	Content	Follow Up

Exercise7:

Share how creating an event strategy supports your event planning business or brand.

_____

_____

Why are public relations and marketing important?

_____

_____

Have you tried advertisements? Have you been successful?

_____

_____

Developing Event Planning Goals

Developing SMART Goals

Many of the steps that you take to develop your event planning business goals can also be used to thoroughly create your client event planning goals. Event planning goals are an important step in planning and hosting an ultimate event.

These goals help to provide your clients with a clear understanding of their event and the steps that will be taken to execute the event. They also provide clarity for your planning and execution event teams.

Side note: An execution team includes your preferred vendors and partners who will provide essential services for your event. We will discuss preferred vendors later in the book.

Why are goals important in event planning?

Developing SMART goals is fundamental in every business. They allow you the opportunity to develop an actionable plan that measures how well your business is doing in your market.

S- Specific

M- Measurable

A-Attainable

R-Realistic

T-Time

Here is an example:

Goal: Within the next 12 months, x business will

increase sales from $2000 per month to $4000 per month.

Exercise 8: Complete the questions using the example above

1. Is the goal specific? Why or why not?
2. Is the goal measure? Share the part of the goal that makes it measurable.
3. Do you think the goal is attainable?
4. Is the goal realistic?
5. What is the time presented?

Now take time to write 3 goals for your business or your upcoming event idea. Be sure to use the steps above to create your goals.

Why are SMART goals important in your event planning business?

SMART goals provide clear direction and clarity for your event planning business. These goals help you to easily articulate your event planning needs and objectives. It also readies your business to obtain sponsors, loans and other business partnerships. As your business grows, you will see just how important well-developed business goals are to the sustainability of your business.

Event Therapy
No Matter the Time, We're Planning

STEP 5
The Key to Time Management

Creating and Implementing Successful Timelines

Every entrepreneur is busy. We are building a business, planning events, executing events and managing a team while balancing our personal lives. If you are just starting, you may also be working a 9-5 job. It can seriously get overwhelming and feel unmanageable; however, it is manageable if you take proper steps. Everyone has the same 24 hours in the day, so there is nothing limiting your success but proper planning.

1. Be mindful of your schedule.

Do you have a planner or calendar that you use daily to keep up with your daily and weekly tasks? If not I would advise you to get on it quick!! As your business grows so does your to-do lists. I always tell my coaching clients that you are no longer managing your business calendar, but you are also managing your personal calendar, your husband's and your children's calendars and more. It is so easy to feel unbalanced without a proper plan in place.

"Eventpreneurship" is time consuming, but at some point, you will find a system that works best for you. Answer the questions below to begin the processing of developing a system that works best for me.

Answer the questions:

1. What does my month, week, day typically look like?
2. What are the standard activities that must get done?
3. What are the activities that I do for fun?
4. Who are the people that need to be in my life daily?
5. Who are my distractions?
6. What are my distractions?

Think about other questions that you should ask yourself. You are the professor of your life.

Just like your checkbook, balance your 24 hours to ensure your schedule is balanced.

Event Therapy

Time Management Tip- Understand the
Difference Between Urgent and Important.

Once you assess your time and manage your budget, you will have a clearer understanding of the how to achieve your monthly, weekly and daily goals.

2. Be aware of your client schedule

Scheduling and using calendar systems are great ways to manage your time. We simply use Google calendar and Google documents. I use this online system to schedule my daily activities and events. I also send calendar invites to our clients to remind them of our scheduled meeting times and dates. This system also allows us to share our working event budgets, bookings and more with them by providing them access.

If you do not have an online calendar, then a planner will work well.

Diagram 7: Event Therapy Time Budget Sheet Example

Daily	Tasks	Weekly Total time	Monthly	Tasks	Yearly total time
Monday	Sleep: 8hrs Hygiene: 2hrs Meals: 1.5hrs 1. 2. 3		January	Sleep: hrs Hygiene: hrs Meals: hrs 1. 2. 3	Sleep: hrs Hygiene: hrs Meals: hrs 1. 2. 3
Tuesday	Sleep Hygiene Meals		February		
Wednesday	Sleep Hygiene Meals		March		
Thursday	Sleep		April		

	Hygiene				
	Meals				
Friday	Sleep		May		
	Hygiene				
	Meals				
Saturday	Sleep		June		
	Hygiene				
	Meals				
Sunday	Sleep		July		
	Hygiene				
	Meals				
		Total Weekly Time			Total Yearly Time

There are many other calendar systems such as Acuity Scheduling that are great to help clients book consultations or sessions with you.

There are plenty of systems available. It is important to find which works best for you and your business.

3. Be reasonable with client timelines

Developing a client timeline to properly plan and execute an event is crucial to maintaining a positive relationship with your client and team. A client timeline consists of assessing what needs to be done for the event before the 2-week mark for execution. I suggest being complete with your event details at least 2 weeks prior to the event. The client should be made aware of the timeline at the start of planning. Clients should also be aware that maintaining their deadlines is a direct reflection of the completion of tasks.

In addition, I have created a production sheet to help manage the event timeline. The team can access this sheet via Google documents to review event identify and deadlines. They are also able to review event assignments.

Event Therapy

Event Planning is based on a desire, not a need.
Plan accordingly!

4. Determine your source of balance.

Determining your source of balance is important in maintaining a level head during any event planning process. I share with my clients and other event professionals that events are a service. It's a want and a desire. It is not a service that is needed.

The event industry runs high on emotions; you must be able handle the mental and physical stress that takes place.

Earlier I stated that you must be mindful of your schedule. I am reflecting on this idea. If you are mindful of your schedule, your daily tasks and standard activities, then you will be able to better manage and balance your time.

Here are a few ways to balance:

1. *Set office hours.*

Treat your business like a corporate job. With planning, we all understand the time commitment to complete tasks, but you must find a stopping point. Most event planners and designers are over thinkers and over achievers. We challenge ourselves to make every event perfect and we forget to take care of ourselves along the way. This is not okay. There is no such thing as a perfect event, but there is a such thing as a relaxed you.

2. *Control your time.*

Require your clients to schedule a call with you rather than them just calling unannounced. This is an extremely important step, because your time is your money and your peace. If you have an assistant, create a follow up system for your clients that requires them to connect with your assistant during specific office hours.

3. *Manage Emails Properly.* Do not feel pressed to open, read and respond to every email that dings on your phone or electronic device. Answer those messages within 24 hours or during your office hours.

Your balance is strictly up to you. Without systems in place, you will find yourself stressed and overwhelmed by this business.

Tips to Planning our Time

Time budget. Just like money, we must assess and budget our time to run a successful event business.

1. Understand the difference between urgent and important.
2. Simply put, what is negotiable and what is non-negotiable? What results will I receive from completing this task?
3. Determine your daily, weekly, monthly and yearly tasks.

Here, I always ask the question: What is due today, tomorrow, end of the month or year? Your tasks are directly correlated to your business plan goals.

<u>Stress Relief Exercises</u>

Deep Breathing- How to effectively reduce stress using deep breathing

https://www.helpguide.org/articles/stress/relaxation-techniques-for-stress-relief.htm

1. Sit comfortably with your back straight. Put one hand on your chest and the other on your stomach.

2. Breathe in through your nose. The hand on your stomach should rise. The hand on your chest should move very little.

3. Exhale through your mouth, pushing out as much air as you can while contracting your abdominal muscles. The hand on your stomach should move in as you exhale, but your other hand should move very little.

4. Continue to breathe in through your nose and out through your mouth. Try to inhale enough so that your lower abdomen rises and falls. Count slowly as you exhale.

There are stress relief exercises that are helpful in managing emotions.

Event Therapy
The Power of Your Network is Fundamental to the Success of your Business

STEP 6
How Do I Secure Preferred Vendors?

Testimonial:

"Our experience with Charessa and SC Visionary Planning & Production Services have always been wonderful. Charessa and staff are truly organized professionals who have always treated us with respect with constant communication prior to, during, and after all events! We are proud to be a partner and highly recommend SC Visionary Services for all your event planning needs."- Miles Smith, The Dj Team @thedjteam

Every event planning company should create a list of preferred vendors. Preferred vendors are businesses such as: caterer, DJ, lighting and sound, etc., that you have created a relationship with and may be able to offer a deal to you for your clients. One of the reasons why clients hire event planners is to be able to secure better deals. When they see that you do an amazing job and you can find deals for them, they are more likely to continue working with you.

Let's break down ways to secure your preferred vendors.

Networking

Networking is top on our list for any business to grow. We find that who you know will take you to many heights in your business. Some great ways of networking include going to various events in your city to meet others. However, networking should be strategic. Know what your purpose in going to the event is and who you would like to meet while you are there. Do your research. Know your target. In addition, attending event planning conferences and seminars such as the SC Ultimate Event Planning Workshop Series and the Bridal Planning Seminar are two great events to attend. Be sure to choose events that make sense to your brand and your target market.

Build relationships.

Networking extends much farther than going to these events or participating in various programs. You must begin to build relationships with those that you have networked with. Be sure to email everyone who you have connected with within 48 hours of meeting them. Offer to sit down for lunch or coffee. Begin building the relationship and see how you may be able to support them in their efforts. Remember it's not just about what you want from them, but more so what you can help them with. The key is showing your value to them.

Work with them at least two times.

Everyone knows that conversations can only take you so far in building relationships with your vendors. It is important to check references and maybe even attend an event that they are participating in. Once you feel comfortable about the vendors work and work ethic, think about hiring them for your next event. I suggest hiring them and working with them at least twice before adding them to them to you preferred vendor list.

Know your target populations.

Lastly, know your target population. Your vendors should be marketable to your target. This is very important for your client and your vendor. It does not make sense to have a DJ who only provides classical music if your target market are small social birthday parties. Think wisely when choosing your vendors.

Event Therapy

Budgeting 101- A budget is telling your money where to go instead of wondering where it went

-Dave Ramsey

STEP 7
Budgets, Contracts & Agreements

Why are thorough client budgets, contracts and vendor agreements important?

A client's budget is one of the most important details for every event because it is your foundation. The amount of money that a client would like to spend on their event will determine your choice of vendors, visuals and more. Also, be specific about your event service rate vs. other vendor service rates. I have included a budget sheet at the end of this chapter.

Securing vendors and contractors also means that you must develop legal binding vendor agreements and contracts. I would suggest sitting down with your lawyer to draw up these forms.

Let's discuss why client contracts and vendor agreements are important.

Every business lives through its contracts and agreements. A contract is a binding document that secures you and your client throughout the business relationship. It is a document that indicates when, where and how the services will be rendered. It also notes the cost of the services that are rendered. Contracts should be reviewed with your client in its entirety before signing.

Review the below scenario:

Betty, a planner with C & S Events is hired to plan and execute an annual gala for an entertainer. The clients provide their budget, number of people and their event expectations. Betty shares that her company can properly execute the details of the event and verbally charges the client $3000 for the services. Once the deposit of 50% is paid, Betty and her team begins working on planning right away. One week before execution Betty approaches her client to obtain the remaining balance before the day of the event. The clients share that she has made the complete balance of $1500 and would not be paying any additional amounts.

Exercise 9:

In your words, share your thoughts on Betty's situation and what you think she should do?

_____

_____

The above scenario has happened time and time again between planners and clients. The event planner never secured the rate of $3000 in a legal document and would most likely have difficulty proving her case.

A thorough contract details all of the services that will be rendered, the approximate number of staff, time spent, cancellation process, etc., should be clearly noted in the contract with your client; this is like your vendor agreements.

Event planning companies often have secured preferred vendor agreements that includes a special rate for the clients and an incentive for the planner. The special rate and the incentives should be documented in the agreement. I would not suggest the idea that "if it's written in the email then I am safe." I have heard this argument often; however, I am not a lawyer and I would better bet my chances on a legal document than an email. By the way, always consult with legal counsel for proper contracts and agreements.

In the previous chapters, we hinted at cost for event services. This is a touchy subject because it is one of the most difficult areas of event planning. How much should you charge for event services is widely dependent on the type of event services that you provide. It also depends on your target populations, geographic location and size of your business. What services can you provide for your client? What is your company rating?

Below are a few methods of how to charge:

1. Hourly

Hourly rates range from $75-$150 an hour or more depending on the type of event you are executing, geographic location and experience. It can be difficult to gauge your potential billable time for the client and may result in charging additional amounts.

2. Percentages

Most planner's charge 15%-20% of the entire client budget for large scale events plus a service fee. For example, if the client full budget is $35,000, then the cost of services will be $7,000 (20%) plus $2000 service fee. Your business pay will equal to $9,000.

3. Packages

It is always great to have special event packages available. This allows your potential clients to note what services are provided and at what starting rate. For example, a small gala with 150 or more guests may start at $3500. This rate does not include the cost of design or décor materials. Be sure that your client understands each deliverable noted in the contract.

4. Flat Rates

Flat rates are often provided to ongoing clients who are executing the exact same event monthly. They are often put on a retainer for 3-6 months for x number of events during that time frame.

5. A La Carte

A la carte rates are for the additional services that a planner may offer to a client i.e. coaching, graphic designs, etc. This is a great way to ensure that the client experiences a one stop shop for all of their event planning service needs.

Combination of Package Rate and Percentages

On any occasion, planners may result to a combination of percentages and hourly rates. This is mostly seen in producing large award shows or projects that require a lot of time and support services.

Unless otherwise discussed, your fees do not include design elements such as decor. Clients generally have a separate budget for design which is to include centerpieces, drapes, lighting & special effects, table linen and more. Most clients will request that you purchase or rent these items for them to take advantage of vendor discounts.

Exercise 9: How to Measure Up!

How do I compete with others in my market?

1. Know your market
2. Stay in your lane
3. Be unique
4. Review your competitors pitch
5. Don't compete

Take 10 minutes to think about your business and its competition. What about your business is unique and will best engage your target market?

Diagram 8: Sample Budget Sheet

Category	Projected Subtotal	Actual Total
Venue		
Food & Beverage		
Decor		
Event Programming		
Entertainment		
Event Documentation		
Event Travel		
Guest services		
Communication		
Registration		
Marketing		
Public Relations		
Social Media		

Advertising		
Sponsors		
Logistics		

Event Therapy

An Event is not over until everyone stops talking about it.

STEP 8
Maintaining Ongoing Clients

How to Maintain Ongoing Clients

As I have shared in the previous chapters, it is important to be yourself when identifying your target market and your specialty. It is also important to simply be yourself with your clients. Your clients fall in love with you sometimes before they fall in love with your work. This may be the simplest step of event planning, but it could also be difficult. Here is why:

Like I said clients fall in love with you so you must look at the relationship with clients like a marriage or like you are "going steady." Simply put, you must court your client before and after that initial date or in our case event. Make sure that you get to know the clients event desires and their needs. Show them respect and position yourself as the expert in your conversation. You want to build authentic rapport and trust with your clients.

1) Be yourself.

Always be authentic. Your ongoing clients would appreciate hiring someone that they can trust and understand.

2) Produce great work.

This is number one. The quickest way to lose a client is to produce unsatisfactory work. You are your clients' employee and you have to be sure that you are producing your very best each time that you work with them. It is easy to get comfortable with ongoing clients but always remember they are still your client.

3) Ensure that they believe in your brand.

Clients that believe in your brand will continue to hire and refer you and your services out to others. Networking is key in any business and the most profitable networking strategy is word of mouth. Your clients will support you if they believe in your brand.

4) Make sure they feel secure.

Clients have to trust that you can do the job. They have to be clear that you are going to meet each deliverable noted in their contract.

5) Be knowledgeable.

The last thing that the client needs to think is that you do not know how to produce their vision.

6) Remain positive.

Yes! Remain a positive source for your client. Hosting an event can be difficult and emotionally draining. Your clients need to know that you have their back at all times.

7) Acknowledge the client as an individual & vision expert

Your client is not money. Your client is an individual or business with a true vision that they would like to make a reality with ease. They are experts in their vision and you are there to assist them with developing and executing a flawless event.

Client testimonial.

Working with Charessa of SC Visionary Planning & Production Services was such a great, memorable experience. An expert in her field, she brought my imagination to reality, the quality of service unmatched. – Courtney Munford, Owner of Black Chef's Network

STEP 9
Understand Event Day Do's and Don'ts

Event day is full of excitement, anxiety and more excitement!! This is the day that all your hard work will be viewed by your client and their guests! It is your movie premiere!

To be brutally honest, if you have not found peace in your event design and logistical plan your event day will SUCK for you and your client. I always say...you are as good as your last event, so make every event the best event ever!

With all of the event day excitement, every event planner must remember that safety is most important. Your event stage manager or production manager is responsible for making sure proper exit signs are posted, outlets are noted and working and clients and participants feel secure.

Let's talk about a few event day don'ts! ☹

On event day, you will spend a lot of time preparing for the clock to strike event time. You are setting up, organizing vendors, placing documents, positioning speakers, rehearsing with entertainment, accepting phone calls, answering questions... you name it you may be doing it. But this is too much. Here are three big event day don'ts:

1.   Arriving late.

There is no explanation for this. If you and your team arrive late on your event day, you risk chopping out a large chunk of time for set up and rehearsal! Most venues allow 1-2 hours to set up your event. This is not a lot of time if you have structures to build, rehearsal, organizing of your team and event essentials.

2.   Not having a task assignment sheet for your staff!

You have prepared your team for 90 days or more to plan and design an amazing event. Be sure to allow them to work the plan. Many event planners find themselves attempting to do everything rather than trusting their team to execute the plan. This is overwhelming and can cause the event logistics to fail. "Too many hands in the cookie jar gets nothing done!" If you have volunteers for your event you must also create a volunteer assignment sheet with your volunteer coordinator. You will be surprised at the amount weight that will be lifted from your shoulder if you simply have task assignments.

3.   Attitude, Unpleasant, not hospitable

As previously mentioned, the event industry is an emotional service. Clients invest a lot of money in your services and in the crafting of the event. Each team member should be trained and ready to handle clients and their guests with a positive attitude and a smile. Clients are expecting all positive energy through the end of their event. Remember you want a satisfactory rating from your client and their guests. Furthermore, you would love for your clients to repeat service with you.

Exercise 10:

What are some other event don'ts?

_____

_____

_____

Event Do's 😊

There are so many event day do's, so I will provide my top 5

1. Be prepared to work hard. Every event takes a strong leader and a strong team that is prepared for each event element. This includes those event issues that pop up like a bartender being tardy, a speaker not showing or even the venue temperature. Each of these issues may hinder an event, but if you are prepared to tackle these areas then you will be successful.

2. Inspect each room that will be used during your event. Take photographs and notes with the venue coordinator.

This helps to avoid potential charges from the venue after your event. In addition, photographing your event before, during and after is a good way to build your portfolio.

3. Make sure your event vendors are knowledgeable of the event timeline and expectations on the day of your event. All vendors should know the correct time of arrival, execution and close out. It is important to provide a copy of the timeline or run of show to your vendor.

4. Always be courteous to client, guests and vendors.

5. Maintain safety.

Event Therapy

If you want something you've never had, you
must be willing to do something
you've never done.

-Thomas Jefferson

STEP 10
Self-Care

Event planning and production can be demanding on planners. It is important to provide self-care strategies and tactics that will help you and your team balance your time and maintain healthy habits.

What ignites the specific need for self-care is different for everyone. Eventpreneurs are faced with so many challenges of the day that range from managing staff, closing deals, planning events and personal activities. There is a constant strain to complete tasks which can trigger stress and anxiety. It is important for you to assess your body and understand when you should take a break. As planners, or in many cases "Perfect Patty's," you become so consumed with providing the perfect event or production for the client that you forget to take care of yourself.

Not taking care of yourself is unhealthy and can lead to physical and mental challenges. In turn, these strategies may impact your relationship with your team and negatively affect your health and more.

"Don't be too busy trying to be the Jack or Jackie of all trades. Become the master of a few! Learn to delegate and set boundaries for the people and roles that you manage.
- Dr. Tiffany Lowe Payne.

I have mentioned a few times that the event industry, though awesome, is an emotional industry. You position yourself to be the support system for your client and that could mean that they will share their darkest moments with you during the event planning process. Processing these moments with your client could lead to challenging emotions within yourself. Having self-care strategies and techniques that you could use to debrief from your calls will be important.

Consequently, communication with your client is important when and if you feel that you placed in a situation that is beyond your scope of expertise. Be careful to not compromise your business relationship with your clients. I would suggest that you develop a plan of action to handle these types of situations.

Event Therapy: 7 Strategies of Self Care

7 Strategies of Self Care

1. Always take time for your family and friends.
2. Plan with you, your team and your client in mind.
3. Eat at least 3 healthy meals a day and exercise regularly.
4. Provide yourself with a spa day.
5. Plan ahead of schedule.
6. Understand the worst, but expect the best from your client relationships.
7. Have fun.

Be sure to add #7 to your daily calendar! It is truly a must.

The above strategies should help you to balance who you are as a professional. Wedding and special event planners often deal with high stress situations due to the nature of the events. Weddings and special events can be emotional events for clients, so building positive relationships with the client during pre-event work is important. Be sure to understand their personality and always promote and accept respect.

Event Therapy
Once you can identify who you are and what
you are good at doing, your business will grow.

Bonus Step
Safety is priority!

Funny now but not so much then...

Be sure to have a safety plan

So, when I first started hosting internal events (events planned and produced for my brands The Table Talk Series and Charge Up Campaign) I was so excited to have products to give to our guests. I had pretty, crisp white gift bags and beautiful pink tissue paper nicely fluffed in the bags. I thought it would be cute to place the bags on the table rather than the chairs (ha, why did I think this was ok). Now the tables were really cute but the one thing that I also added to the table were beautiful floating candles and votives. Now, are you following me? Well, everything was going well and looked great!! Go me! Until one of the guests decides to take the pink tissue paper out to look inside the bags while the event was going on. I looked up and yep... you are right ... Flames!!!! I noticed this travesty at the right time and was able to put the fire out before the restaurant owner noticed and the rest of the guest panicked! Thank heavens, right? Well, right now our rented pink satin linen was damaged and I had just learned a few lessons:

There should always be an emergency plan in place.

There should always be a safety plan in place i.e. what happens if, when you should. remove your clients or participants.

Be sure to have general liability insurance.

Always be mindful of your table design and the use of open flames! Your clients or participants are not as cautious as you!

Moment of Reflection

In this book, we have discussed several areas on ultimate event planning. If you follow these steps, you will be better able to create and maintain a successful event planning business.

It is important to note that the event planning and production industry is a desire and not a need-based industry. You must be prepared to work hard and follow essential steps to be successful in a forest of many event planning companies. The first step is understanding who you are as a planner. What do you like about the industry and what are you good at doing? Your target population will be attracted to your qualities and will hire you because of how you make them feel. Your services will be executed by a team of planners, volunteers and vendors who must feel supported throughout the planning process. Maintaining positive communication and relationships will help to maintain a viable team and secure ongoing clients and vendor relationships. It is important to protect yourself and your clients by developing contracts and vendor agreements that are created by a lawyer. Event planning is fun and visual but it is also a business that must be ran with business care. I would suggest having an accountant, a lawyer and public relations or marketing professional as mentors and a part of your board of directors. This will greatly reduce what we call event warfare. Mentorship is fundamental in the lifeline of your business because it provides you with someone to talk with about important business factors including proper documentation for services before the day of event. Be sure to always be on time, be prepared and ready to execute an amazing event for your clients. You are only as good as your last event.

Throughout it all, self-care and stress relief strategies will be the core of your success. Anytime you are working with people, you will have to find ways to maintain focus and mental comfort. The event will not work if you have not taken care of yourself. I will suggest planning ahead and taken time away from the planning process. Remember, no matter how intense the event is you must make sure that you are prepared to make it happen. Never neglect yourself during the process.

Be Yourself!

Be positive!

Be Safe!

Communicate Well!

& Simply Have fun!!

Works Cited

http://heidicohen.com/marketing-versus-pr-whats-the-difference/

http://www.dummies.com/business/customers/identifying-your-target-market-in-event-management/

About the Author

Charessa Sawyer is a North Carolina native, Certified Event Planner and Social Worker of over 5 and 10 years, respectively. She is also the CEO of SC Visionary Planning & Production Services as well as founder of the Charge Up Campaign and the Table Talk Series with Simply Charessa.

Charessa is simply a visionary that has dedicated her life to supporting and celebrating others through events and productions with a purpose. As the leader and visionary of SC Visionary Planning & Production Services, she spearheads cause-based campaigns for nonprofits and philanthropists. Charessa is committed to producing events that are fundamental to the growth of those who are reached; she is committed to sharing her knowledge with other planners in efforts to build a collaborative group of event professionals that produce amazing work in their specific industry.

Charessa works with professionals from various industries like public relations, sponsorship management, lighting, sound and more in efforts to provide her coaching clients and event planning clients with a well-rounded and organized team to support their visions. She says that mastering relationships and building networks in business are key to your vision's harvest.

Charessa's faith and spirituality is the basis to her leadership and success in the event and production industry. She empowers her team and clients to create their own lane in a forest of so many. It is that guidance she has received from her own coaches and mentors that she has learned the power of her own visions.

Charessa is always excited to share her knowledge of event planning with her colleagues and up and coming planners. Her personal coaching program, *Event Therapy,* is proven to not only share details fundamental to event growth but also provide therapeutic skills and modalities helpful in managing the high intensity of the field.

Booking Charessa S. for your next event will bring high energy level guidance to securing your next event, knowledge-based event strategies and the therapeutic skills to support all planners with managing emotions related to their event!

Charessa is available for panels, speaking engagements and hosting.

info@scvisionaryservices.com